A Body, Owner's Guide

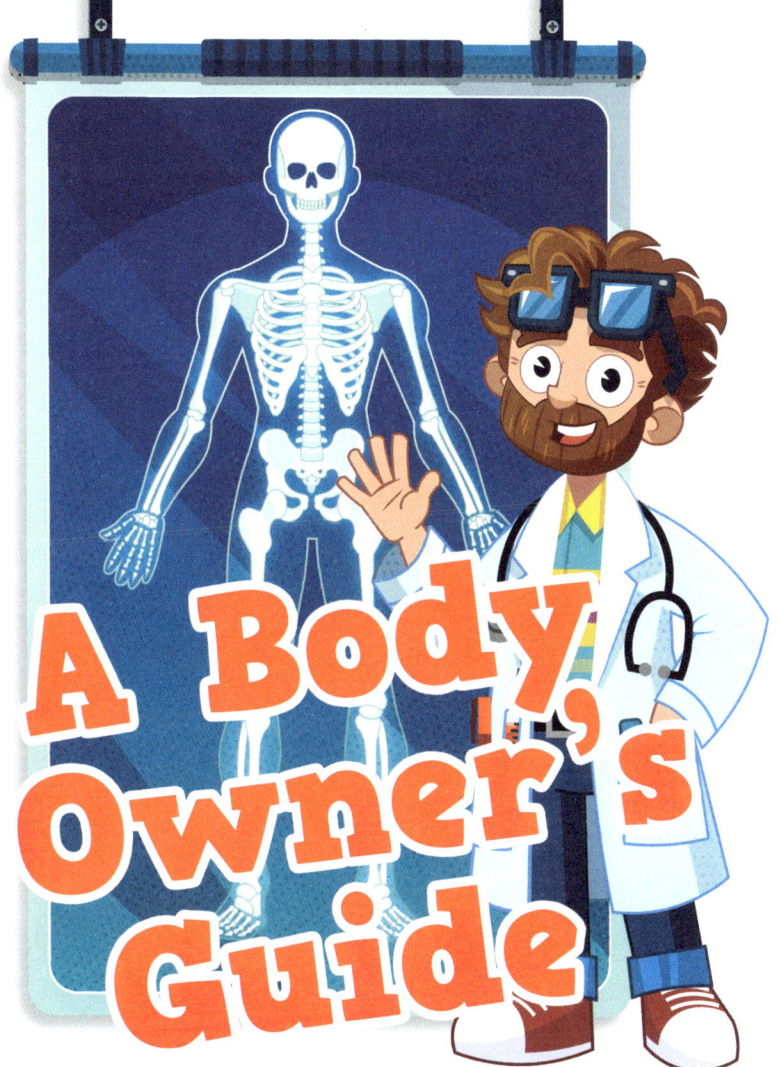

A Body, Owner's Guide

Anita Ganeri

Diego Vaisberg

Collins

Contents

Body maps 2

Chapter 1 What's on the outside? 4

Inside a cell 16

Chapter 2 Bones and moving 18

Record-breaking muscles and bones 30

Chapter 3 Heart, blood and breathing 32

Taking a breath 42

Chapter 4 Munching a meal 44

A great plate? 54

Chapter 5 Brain and nerves 56

Memory skills 68

Chapter 6 Super senses 70

Tricks of the senses 82

Glossary 84

About the author 86

About the illustrator 88

Book chat 90

Body maps

Your body is amazing. It has thousands of different parts, all working together to keep you alive. Here are two maps showing the places we'll visit on this body tour.

On the outside

Inside the body

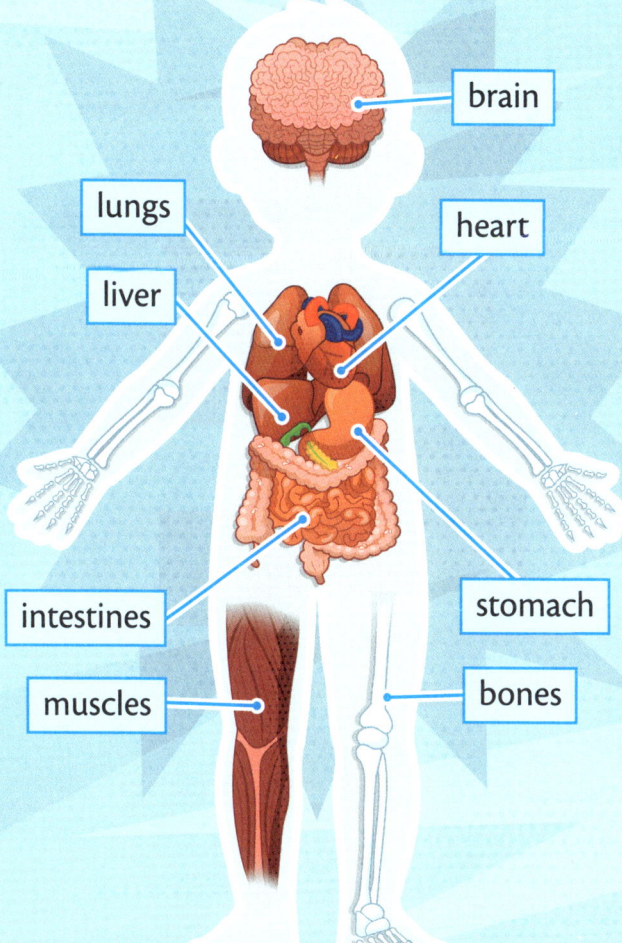

CHAPTER 1
What's on the outside?

Good morning! I'm Dr B. Ody (and yes, I've heard ALL the jokes about my name before).
I'm very pleased to meet you.
I'm delighted to say that I'll be your guide today.

First, a few quick questions.
Do you know what a pupil is?
Or where you'd find your smallest bones? No? Don't worry. Our tour will give you all the answers you need. It will take you right around your body, from your head to your toes, and all the bits in between. You'll soon get to know yourself a lot better – I guarantee it. Before we set off, though, I've got a few announcements to make.

Please listen carefully – they won't take long:

1. There's a body map at the start of this book, in case you get lost.
2. We'll stop for lunch in Chapter 4. It's all about eating a meal.
3. The same goes if you need the toilet. You'll have to wait till Chapter 4, too.
4. If you feel tired, we can take a quick break. It's vital for your body to rest.
5. And finally … Look out for speech bubbles like this one.

Cells: the building blocks of YOU!

Before we get going on our tour, I need to tell you about **cells**. Your body's built from around 17 trillion cells (adults have around 36 trillion!). Sorry, I don't know who counted them all. They are different shapes and sizes, depending on the job they do.

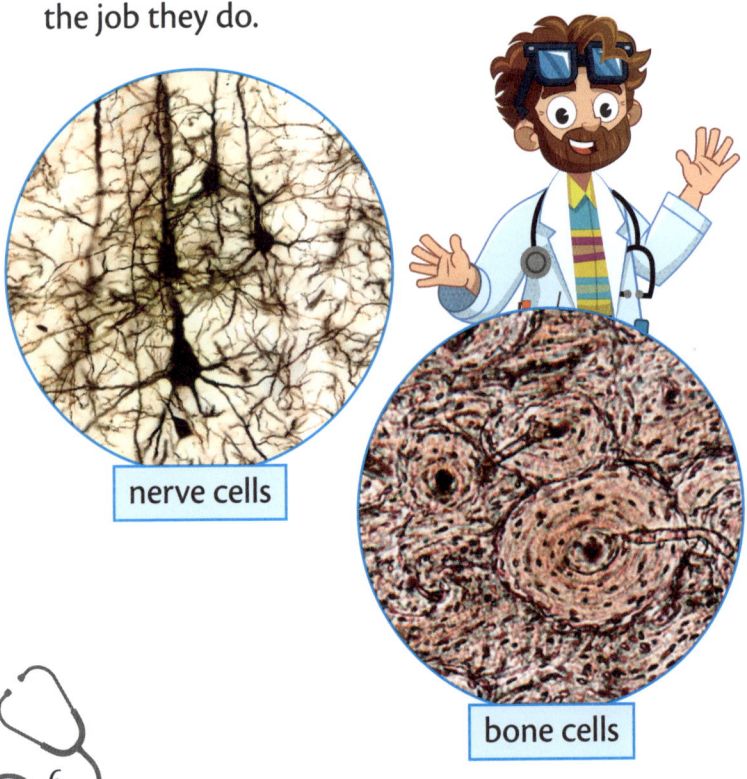

nerve cells

bone cells

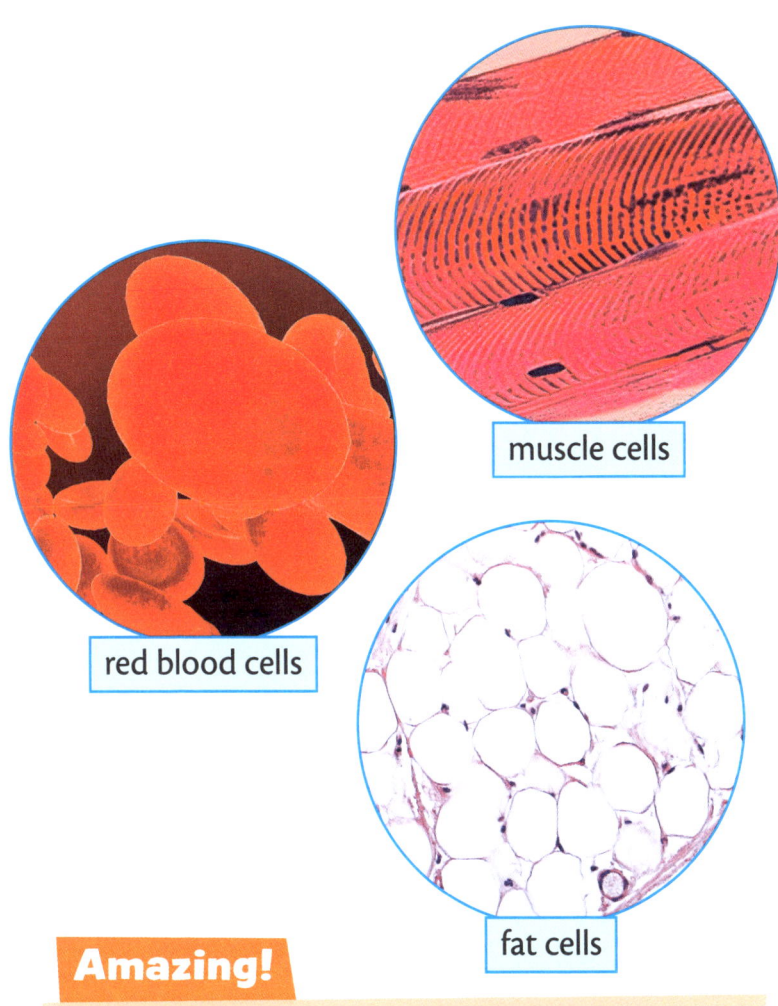

muscle cells

red blood cells

fat cells

Amazing!

Brain and nerve cells can last a lifetime. But the cells lining your **small intestine** (the long tube in your tummy) only live for around three days. There's no need to worry, though. New cells grow and take their place.

Tissues, organs and systems

Cells work as part of a group. Groups of cells that do the same job are called "tissues". No, they're not the type of tissue you blow your nose on. These tissues form parts of your body, including your skin, blood and muscles.

Groups of tissues work together to make body organs. These are parts of your body like your liver, heart and lungs.

Groups of organs join up to form body systems, such as your digestive system (the parts of your body that break down and use food when you eat).

All of the different systems work with each other to build your all-singing, all-dancing, brilliant body.

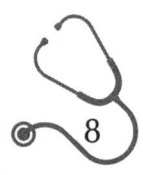

Super skin

Everybody ready? Right, let's get going. First stop on our tour is your super-strong, super-stretchy skin. You can't miss it – you're covered in it from head to toe. In most places, it's around two millimetres thick, but it's thinner on your eyelids, and thicker on the soles of your feet. And it's very useful.

Dr B.Ody's top tip

If you cut yourself and a **scab** grows, don't pick it. (Even if you *really, really* want to.) The scab works like a sticking plaster, keeping the wound covered up, until your skin heals.

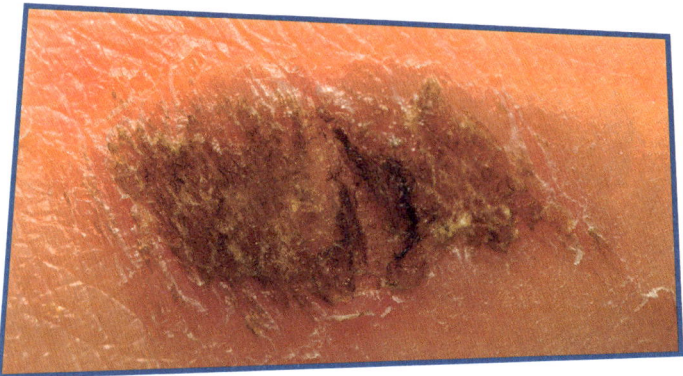

What does skin do?

- It holds your body together.
- It protects you from the harmful rays of the sun.
- It keeps out water and **germs**.
- It cools you down by sweating.
- It warms you up by getting goose bumps.
- It lets you touch and feel things.
- It is where your hair and nails grow from.

Under your skin

The skin you can see is called the epidermis. It's made from dead skin cells. The layer below that is the dermis. This is the layer that makes new skin cells, sweat and oil (to keep your skin soft). It's packed with **blood vessels** and **nerves**. It's also where your hair grows from.

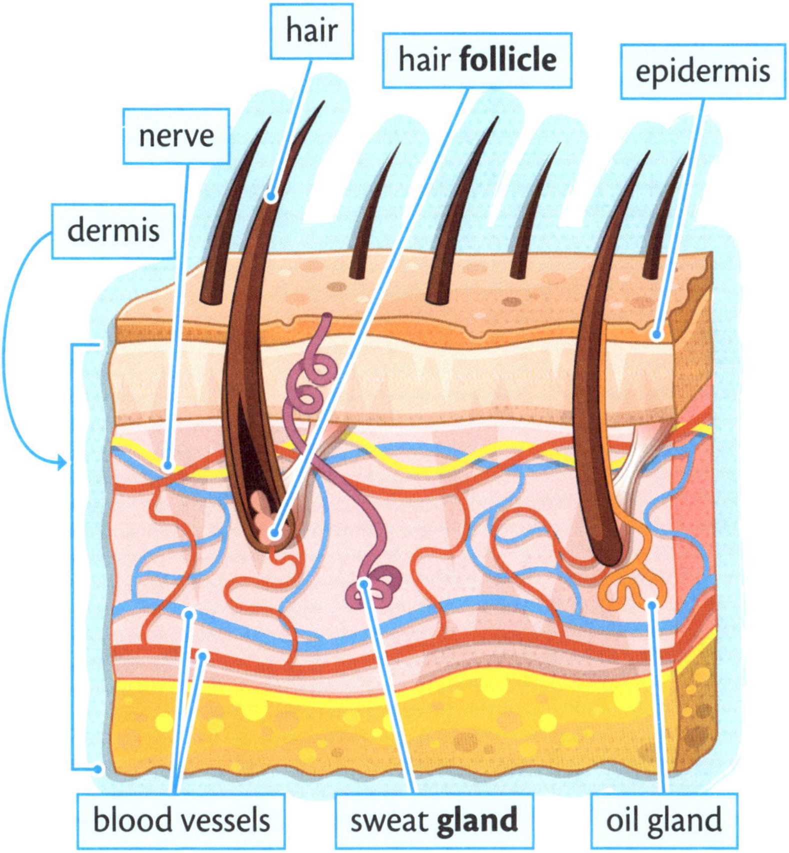

You shake off millions of old, dead skin cells every day. But where do they go? Some of them are in all that dust in your bedroom …

Hair-raising facts

Millions of hairs grow from your skin. They're made from a very tough material, called keratin. Keratin is also in your nails, as well as rhinos' horns and horses' hooves.

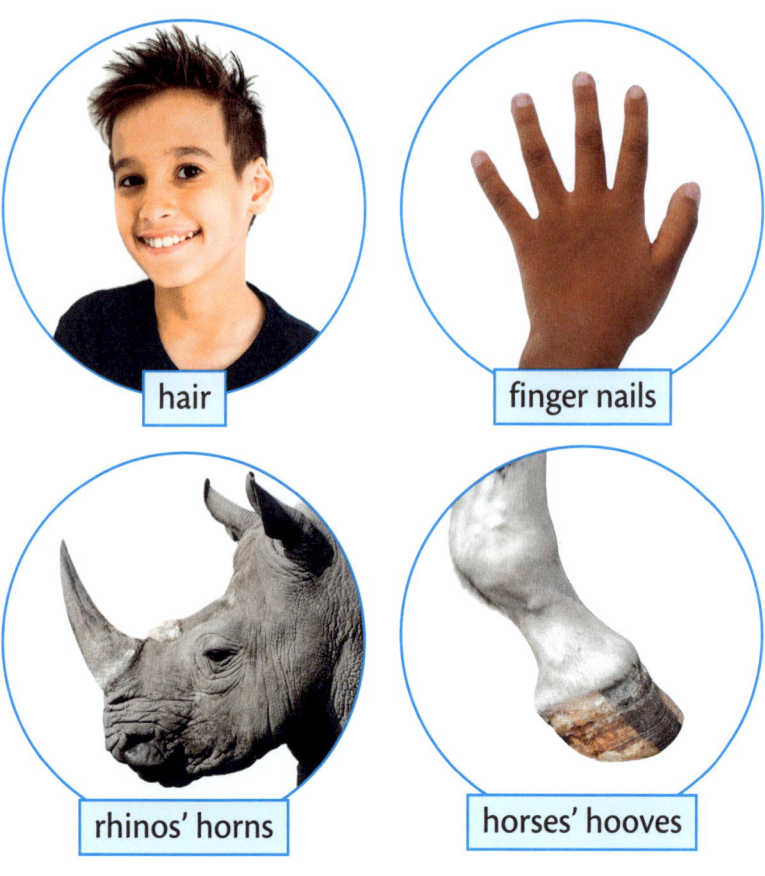

hair

finger nails

rhinos' horns

horses' hooves

Here's what hairs do …

hairs on your head: protect your **scalp** from the sun

eyebrows: stop sweat and water dripping into your eyes

eyelashes: keep dust and dirt out of your eyes and shield your eyes from the sun

Amazing!

Hundreds of tiny, spider-like **mites** live on your eyelashes. They feed on oil from your skin. It sounds gross but they're harmless, and almost everybody has them.

Nail-biting notes

Your nails grow from the skin at the end of your fingers and toes. Like hair, they're made from dead cells. That's why it doesn't hurt when you cut them. Nails are hard and tough to protect your fingertips. They're also handy if you've got an itch ...

fingerprint

Amazing!

The skin on your fingertips is covered in tiny **ridges**, called fingerprints. No one else in the world has the same pattern of fingerprints as you.

cuticle

fingernail

Amazing!

Your nails grow slowly, around a millimetre a week. They speed up in summer, and slow down in winter. Your fingernails grow faster than your toenails.

Inside a cell

Most of your cells are too small to see, except under a **microscope**. But don't worry if you don't have a microscope handy. Here's what the insides of a typical cell might look like:

> **Key**
>
> **1** A very thin skin around the outside of the cell. It lets **oxygen** and food into the cell. It lets waste out of the cell.
>
> **2** The cell's control centre. It carries instructions that tell the cell how to work and grow.
>
> **3** A jelly that fills most of the cell. It does many jobs to keep the cell alive.
>
> **4** The cell's power stations. They supply the cell with energy from food.

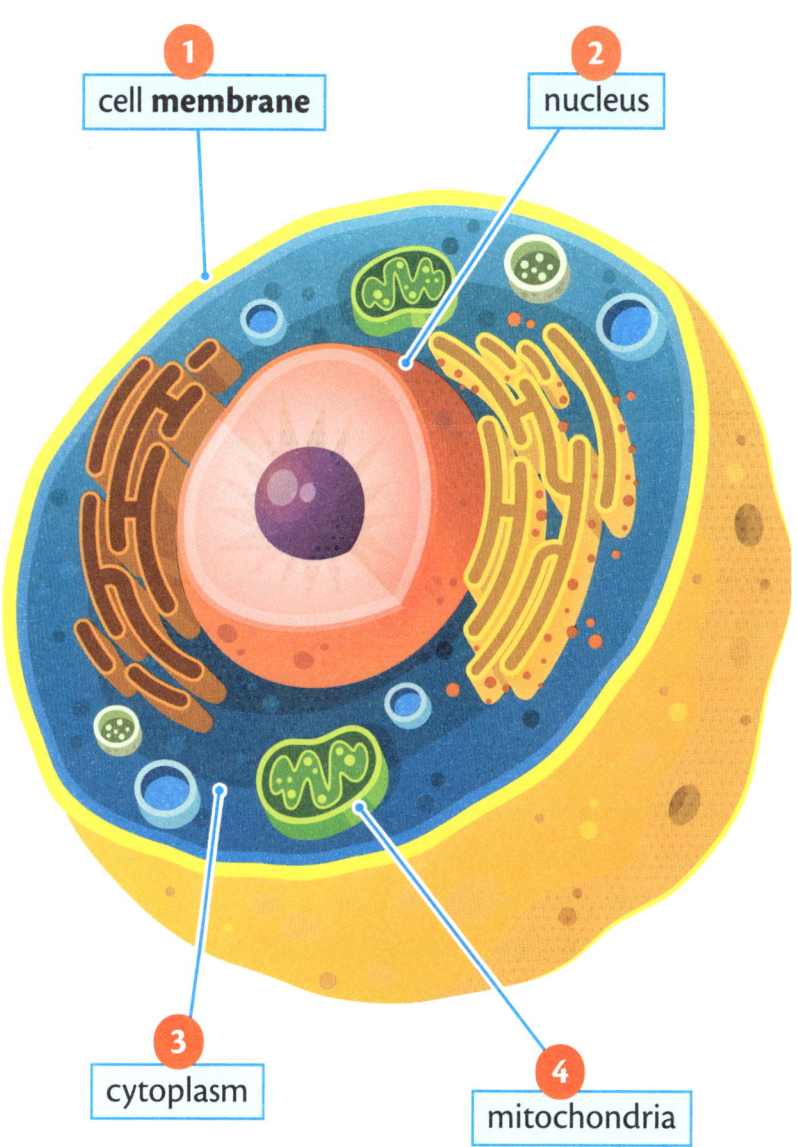

CHAPTER 2
Bones and moving

Right, everyone, there's no time for dawdling. We've still got lots of places to go and lots of things to see. Luckily, this chapter's all about being on the move. So, please follow me. We're heading inside to explore your skeleton.

Skeleton superpowers

Your skeleton is made of more than 200 bones which fit together inside you like a giant 3-D jigsaw. Your skeleton is like a frame that holds your body up and keeps it in shape. Without it, you'd collapse in a big, blobby heap which would make a terrible mess. Your skeleton also protects **delicate** bits, like your brain and heart. And, last but not least, it works with your muscles to get you moving.

Amazing!

You've got seven bones in your neck. That's the same number as a giraffe!

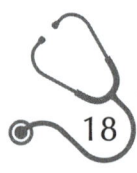

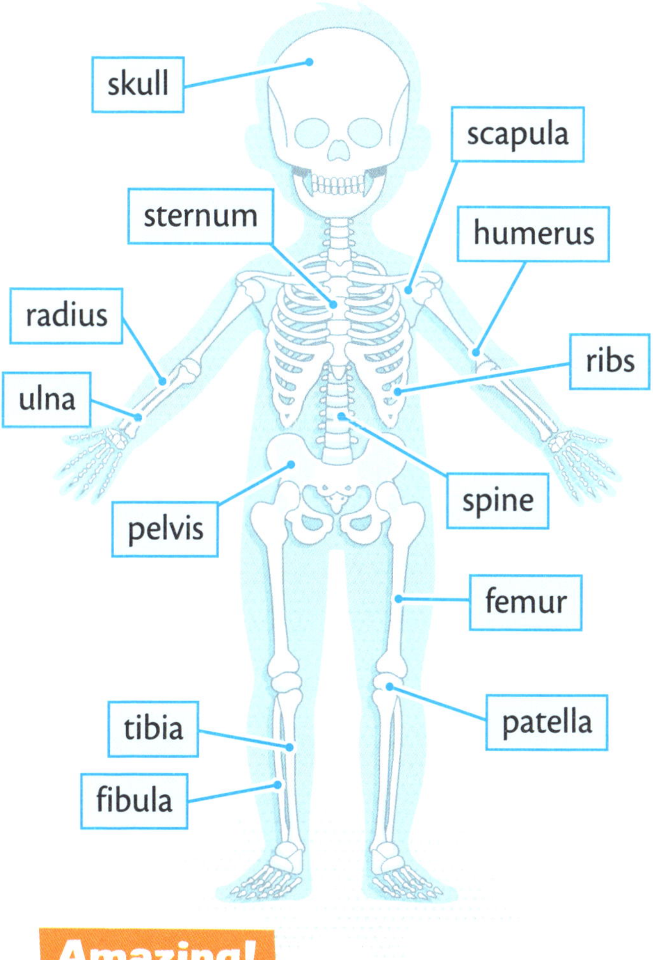

skull
scapula
sternum
humerus
radius
ribs
ulna
spine
pelvis
femur
tibia
patella
fibula

Amazing!

There's nothing funny about hitting your funny bone. There's a big nerve that goes round your elbow that REALLY hurts if you bash it.

Build-a-bone

Bones are hard and tough on the outside, and spongy on the inside. They are stronger than steel but much lighter, so you're still able to move around. Some of your big bones are filled with a jelly-like tissue called bone **marrow**. The marrow makes red blood cells.

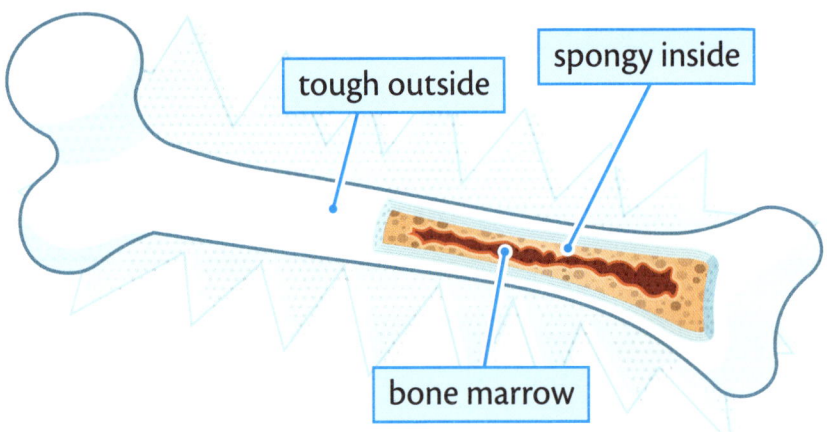

Amazing!

When you're born, your skull has soft patches so it can stretch as your brain grows bigger. As you get older, these soft patches start to join together and turn into hard bone.

Broken bones

Bones are seriously tough but can break sometimes. Luckily, your brilliant body can mend broken bones by itself. If you break a bone, it may take a few weeks for new bone cells to grow over the break. But that should give your friends plenty of time to sign your plaster cast.

Dr B.Ody's top tip

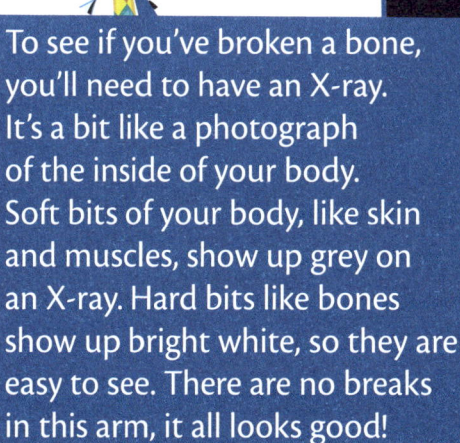

To see if you've broken a bone, you'll need to have an X-ray. It's a bit like a photograph of the inside of your body. Soft bits of your body, like skin and muscles, show up grey on an X-ray. Hard bits like bones show up bright white, so they are easy to see. There are no breaks in this arm, it all looks good!

Moving parts

Joints are the places in your skeleton where two bones meet. You've got around 350 joints, and they let you bend and move. Strong, stretchy straps hold the bones together. Soft pads stop the ends of the bones rubbing. Squelchy liquid around them stops them from creaking.

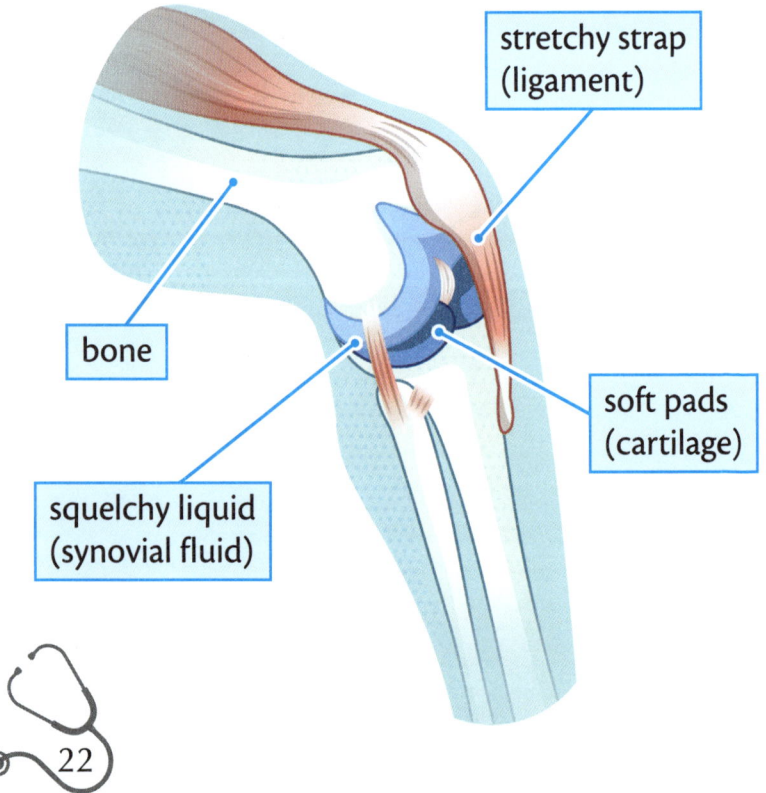

stretchy strap (ligament)

bone

soft pads (cartilage)

squelchy liquid (synovial fluid)

Keep a look out for:

1. Hinge joints

Where:	knees and elbows
How they work:	like door hinges
Movement:	backward and forwards

2. Ball-and-socket joints

Where:	hip, shoulders
How they work:	ball turns in socket
Movement:	all directions

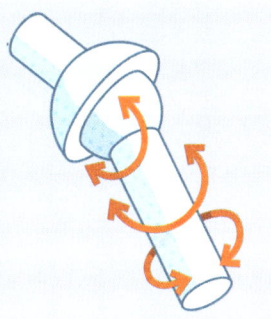

3. Pivot joints

Where:	neck, wrist
How they work:	swivel around
Movement:	side to side

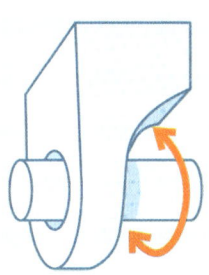

Mighty muscles

You might not have big, bulging biceps like a weightlifter, but you and a weightlifter have both got the same number of muscles. You have muscles all over your body, even in your heart, skin and eyes. They wiggle your ears, stick out your tongue, keep you breathing and make you move.

Muscles are made of bundles of long, thin, elastic threads (fibres). A big muscle has around 2,000 bundles of fibres. Each of these bundles is made of thousands of even finer fibres.

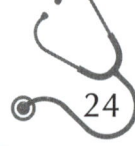

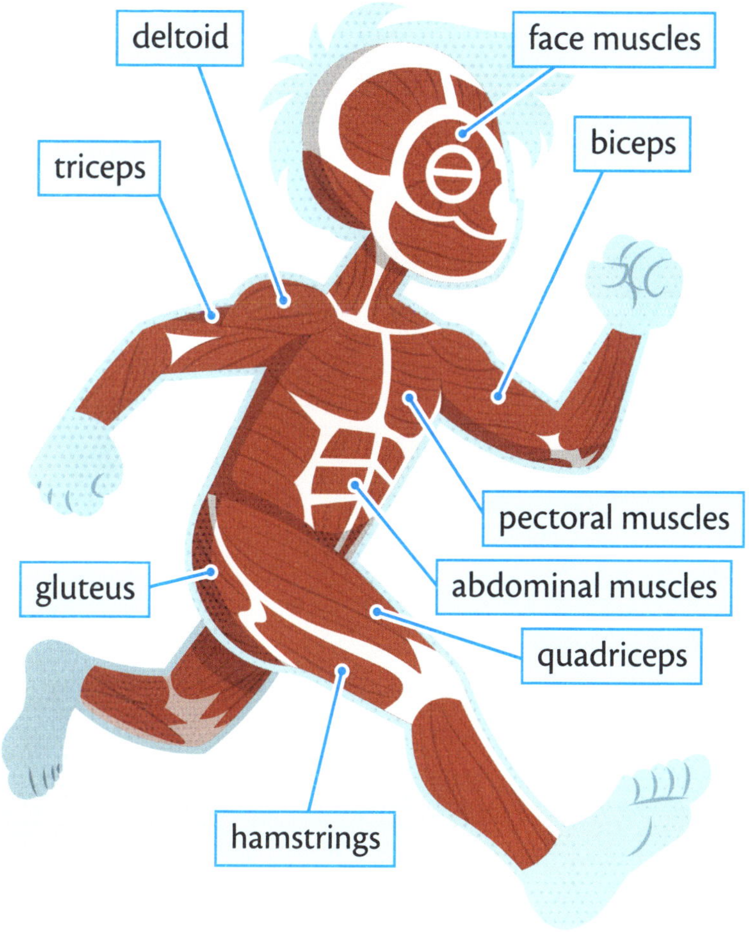
deltoid
face muscles
triceps
biceps
pectoral muscles
gluteus
abdominal muscles
quadriceps
hamstrings

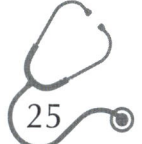

Making a move

Your muscles help your bones to move, so you can do things like run, jump and pick things up. Pairs of muscles work together to move bones. When one muscle pulls the bone, the other muscle relaxes.

Take bending and straightening your arm …

1. Your brain sends messages to your arm.

2. The messages tell your biceps muscle to get shorter.

3. The shortened biceps muscle pulls on your arm bone to bend your elbow.

Amazing!

You've got about 640 muscles, and you need every one of them. After all, it takes about 200 muscles to take a single step forward.

4. Then messages tell your biceps muscle to relax.

5. They tell your triceps muscle to get shorter.

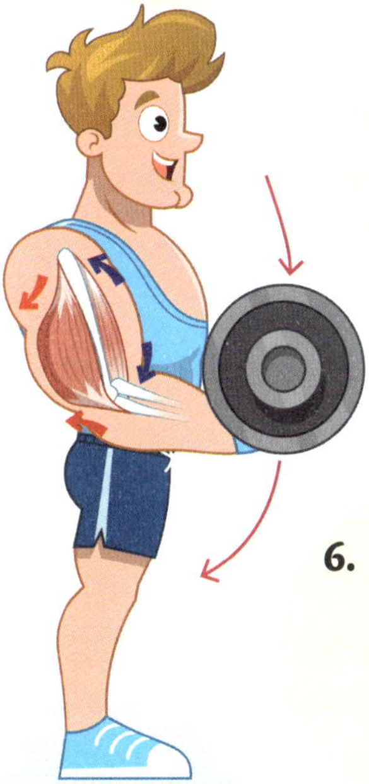

6. The shortened triceps muscle pulls on your arm bone to straighten your arm.

Pulling a face

Not all muscles pull on your bones. Some tug on your skin instead. These are the thin, stretchy muscles in your face that work hard to make you smile, frown, look surprised and stick your tongue out. Your tongue is also a muscle – a big, bendy one that helps you make sounds, eat your food and do tongue-twisting party tricks.

Your hard-working heart is a special kind of muscle. Unlike your other muscles, your heart never gets tired. Night and day, it keeps pumping blood around your body to keep you alive.

Amazing!

The muscles in your eyelids are the fastest workers in your body. They make you blink around 20,000 times a day. Blinking helps make sure your eyes don't dry out. It also keeps them clean.

Dr B.Ody's top tip

Exercise is excellent for keeping your bones and muscles **supple** and strong. You don't have to be super-sporty. Try swimming, scooting, walking, or dancing.

Record-breaking muscles and bones

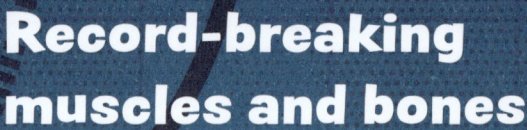

Smallest bone
Name: stapes
Where is it? inside your ear
What does it do? sends sounds into your ears

Biggest bone
Name: femur
Where is it? your thigh
What does it do? helps you stand and move

Biggest muscle
Name: gluteus maximus
Where is it?
your bottom
What does it do?
helps you stand upright and walk

Smallest muscle
Name: stapedius
Where is it?
inside your ear
What does it do?
helps hold ear bones in place

CHAPTER 3
Heart, blood and breathing

Everyone still standing? Don't worry, it'll soon be lunchtime, but we've got a few more stops to make before we have a rest. This way, please, to your heart, blood and lungs.

Beating heart

You'll find your heart in the middle of our chest, slightly to the left and between your lungs. No, I'm afraid it doesn't look like the kind of heart you see on a soppy Valentine's card. It's not pink, and it isn't heart-shaped. It's red and shaped like a pear. It's about the size of your **clenched** fist. Your heart is made of super-strong muscle that pumps blood around your body, and you couldn't live without it.

32

Amazing!

Your hard-working heart pumps around 75 times a minute. That's almost 110,000 (one hundred and ten thousand) times every day. It doesn't stop, even when you're asleep.

In a heartbeat

Each pump of your heart is called a heartbeat. Here's what happens:

1. Blood that has been around your body and used up its oxygen supply, flows into the right side of your heart.
2. Your heart pumps it into your lungs.
3. In your lungs, your blood picks up oxygen.
4. This oxygen-rich blood flows from your lungs into the left side of your heart.
5. Your heart pumps your blood around your body.

Amazing!

An enormous blue whale has a whopping heart. It weighs as much as 600 human hearts and is as big as a piano.

Brilliant blood

Dr B. Ody's top tip

You don't need to see a doctor to check your heart is beating. Press gently on the inside of your wrist, below your thumb. The "throb-throb" you can feel is blood whooshing along. It's called your pulse.

Blood doesn't just slop around your body. It travels along a one-way system of tubes, called blood vessels. They're all over your body, even in your eyes. Blood carries vital supplies of oxygen and food to your cells and takes waste away. It also fights off germs when you're ill.

Amazing!

You've got around 96,000 kilometres of blood vessels. If you could lay them out, end to end, they'd stretch around the world TWICE.

Blood is made from:

- red blood cells – carry oxygen
- white blood cells – fight germs
- platelets (bits of cells) – help blood to form a **clot**
- plasma – watery liquid that carries blood cells and platelets around your body.

You'd need a microscope to see these cells for yourself. Here's what you're looking for …

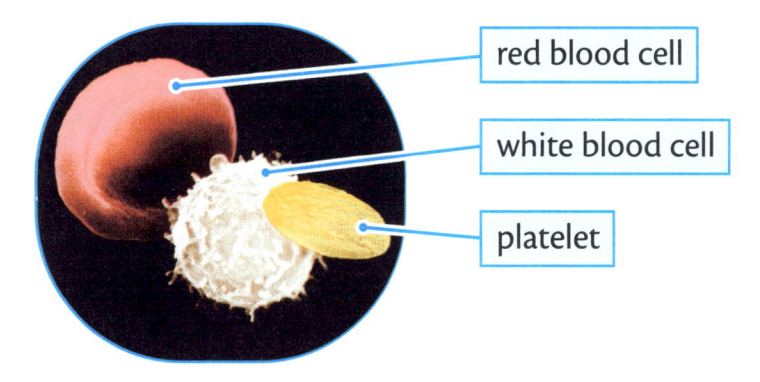

red blood cell

white blood cell

platelet

There are around five million red blood cells in each drop of your blood. It takes them less than a minute to travel all around your body.

Breathing lungs

Sitting on either side of your heart, you've got two lungs. They're like two big spongy bags, and they breathe in oxygen from the air. Humans and all living things need oxygen to be able to survive.

Your blood carries the oxygen around your body to your cells to make them work. Your cells make waste carbon dioxide gas which can be harmful. Your blood picks this up and carries it to your lungs to breathe out.

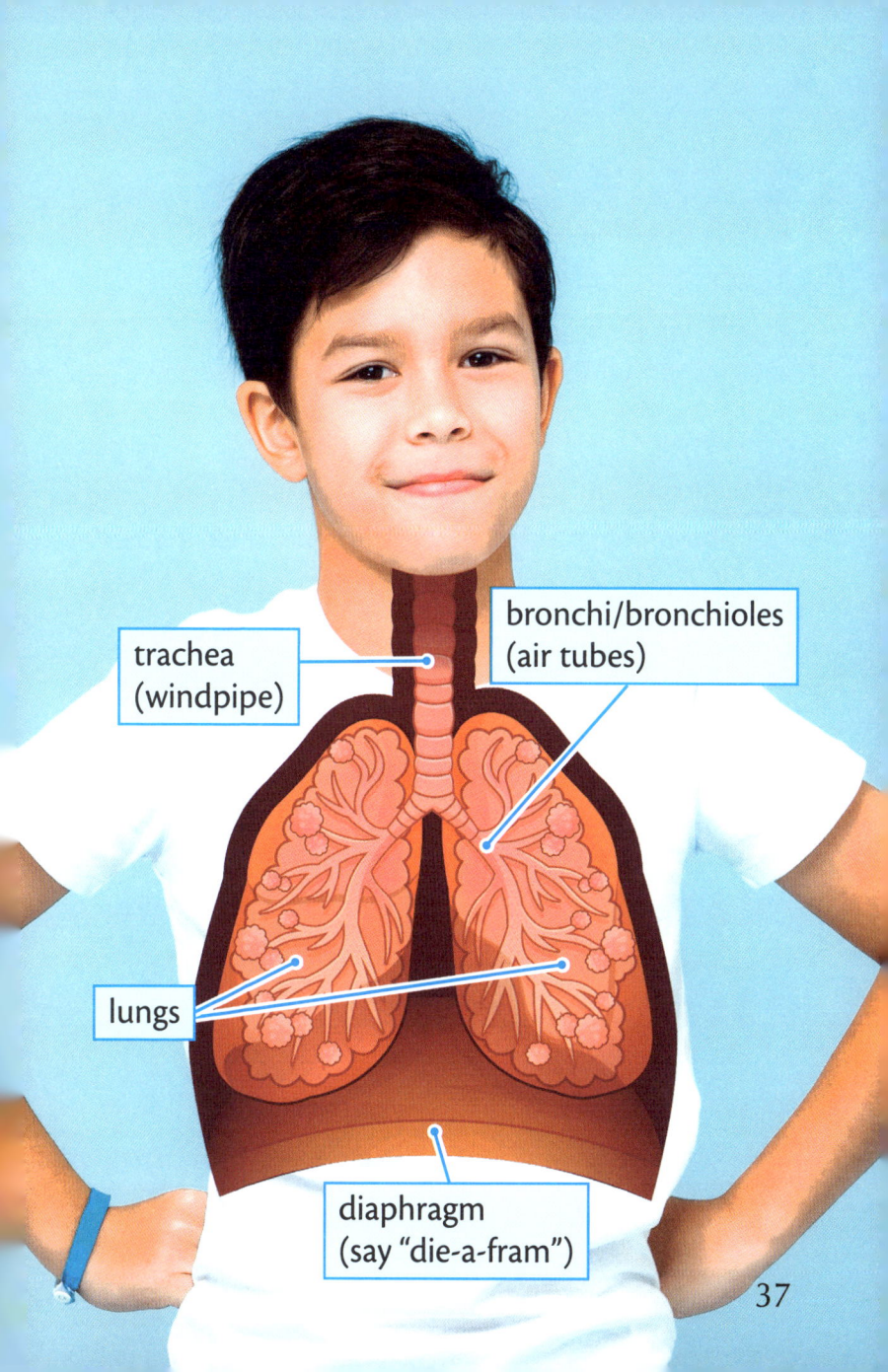

- trachea (windpipe)
- bronchi/bronchioles (air tubes)
- lungs
- diaphragm (say "die-a-fram")

Inside story

The air you breathe in goes down a large tube in your throat, called your windpipe. Then it goes down two smaller tubes into your lungs. In your lungs, the tubes divide into smaller and smaller tubes. There are millions of small tubes, each with an air bag. The air goes into them and fills them up. Each air bag is covered in tiny blood vessels. Oxygen from the air moves from the air bag into your blood through the blood vessels. Then your blood carries it to your cells. The waste carbon dioxide made by your cells travels in the opposite direction. It goes from your cells into your blood, and then to your lungs for you to breathe out.

Amazing!

Sometimes, you feel the need to suddenly take a deep gulp, and YAWWWWWN! Yawning can be catching. Oops, now everyone's started.

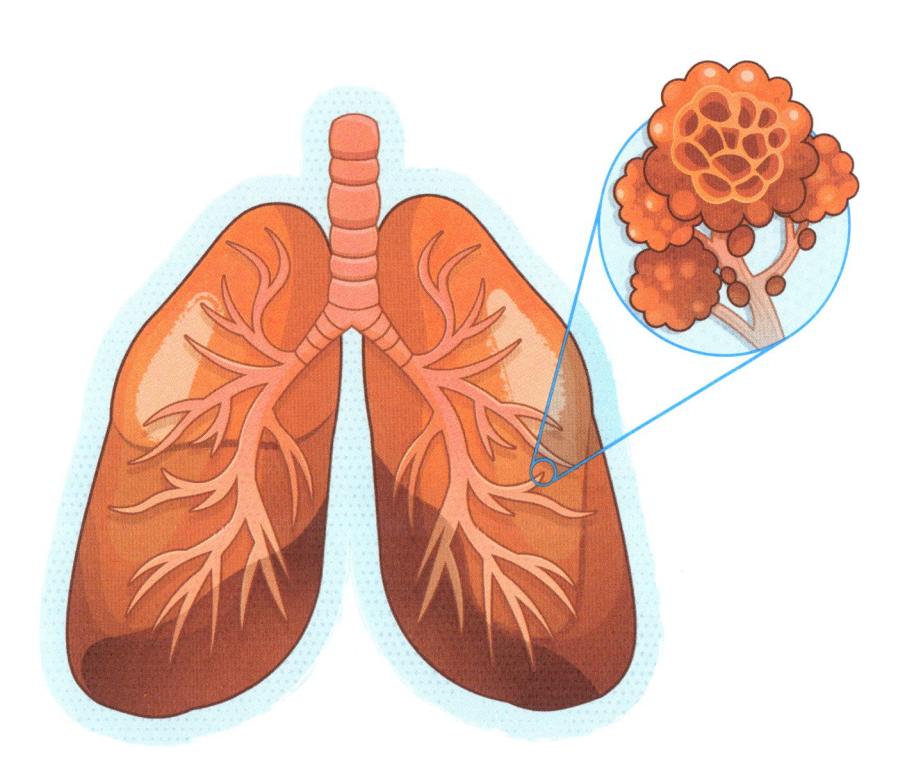

Keeping breathing

Your body can't live without oxygen. That's why breathing is so important. To get enough air into your body, you have to breathe in and out around 20,000 times a day. Luckily, breathing happens **automatically**. So, you don't need to keep telling your body to breathe, and there's no danger you'll forget.

Talking the talk

Birds tweet. Lions roar. But humans are the only animals that are able to say actual words. So, how do we do that? At the top of your windpipe, there's a little opening. Two thin bands stretch across it. The opening is called your larynx (voice box), and the bands are your vocal cords. When you speak, you breathe out and air flows past the cords. The air makes them shake, or vibrate, and make sounds.

Dr B.Ody's top tip

Ever had – HIC! – hiccups? How annoying – HIC! – are they? Hiccups happen when the muscle under your lungs suddenly twitches. This muscle's called your diaphragm. You take a sharp suck of air and – HIC! People have tried all sorts of cures for hiccups, like drinking from the wrong side of a glass or giving someone a fright. But I'd – HIC! – let hiccups – HIC! – clear up on their own. HIC!

Taking a breath

Breathing in ...

1. Air goes in through your nose or mouth and down into your lungs.
2. Your ribs move out. Your diaphragm moves down.
3. This makes your chest bigger and gives your lungs space to fill with air.

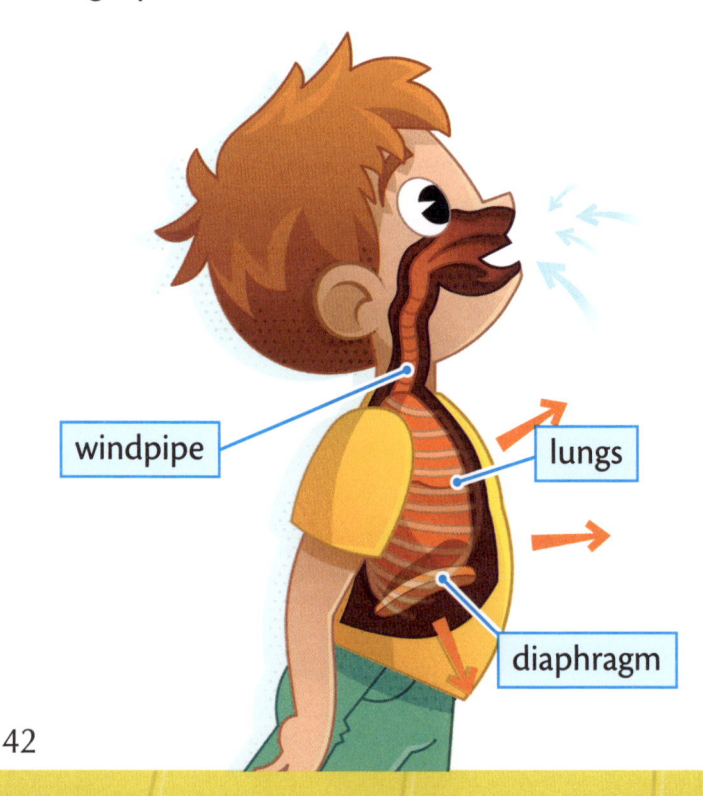

windpipe

lungs

diaphragm

Breathing out ...

1. Your ribs move down. Your diaphragm moves up.
2. This squeezes your lungs and pushes stale air out.
3. The air goes up your windpipe, and out through your mouth or nose.

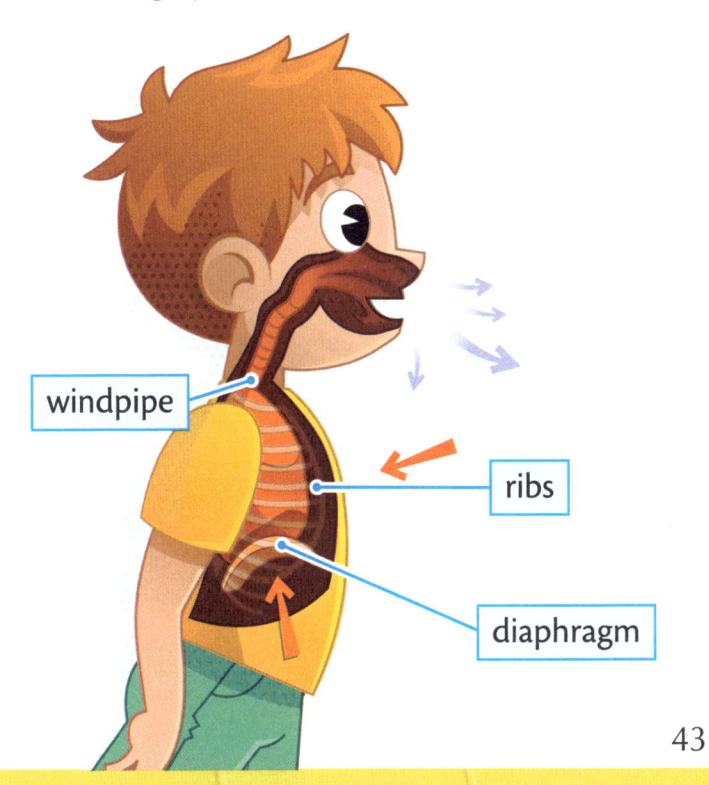

CHAPTER 4
Munching a meal

We're halfway through our tour now, and it's time for that break I promised. Anyone hungry? While you're eating your lunch, I'll talk you through where your food is going. But please put your hand up if you feel sick.

Amazing!

In your lifetime, you'll probably munch your way through around 30 tonnes of food. That's the same as six whole elephants, or a lip-smacking 200,000 sandwiches!

Hunger pangs

Feeling hungry is how your body tells you it's low on energy. Your body gets its energy from food. Food has **nutrients** to help your body mend and grow. But first, food has to be broken down into pieces small enough to be absorbed into your blood. It goes on a long journey through your insides. This process is called digestion. And it starts with your first bite …

Let's follow the journey of digestion …

1. Mouth

In your mouth, your teeth chop and chew your food into smaller pieces. Watery spit mixes with your food to make it slippery and easier to swallow. It also makes your mouth water when you see a yummy meal.

Teeth

Babies usually start off with no teeth at all. But you grow two sets during your lifetime. At around six months, your 20 "milk" teeth start to grow. These start to fall out when you're about five or six years old. They are replaced by your 32 adult teeth. These are different sizes and shapes for chewing, cutting and tearing up food.

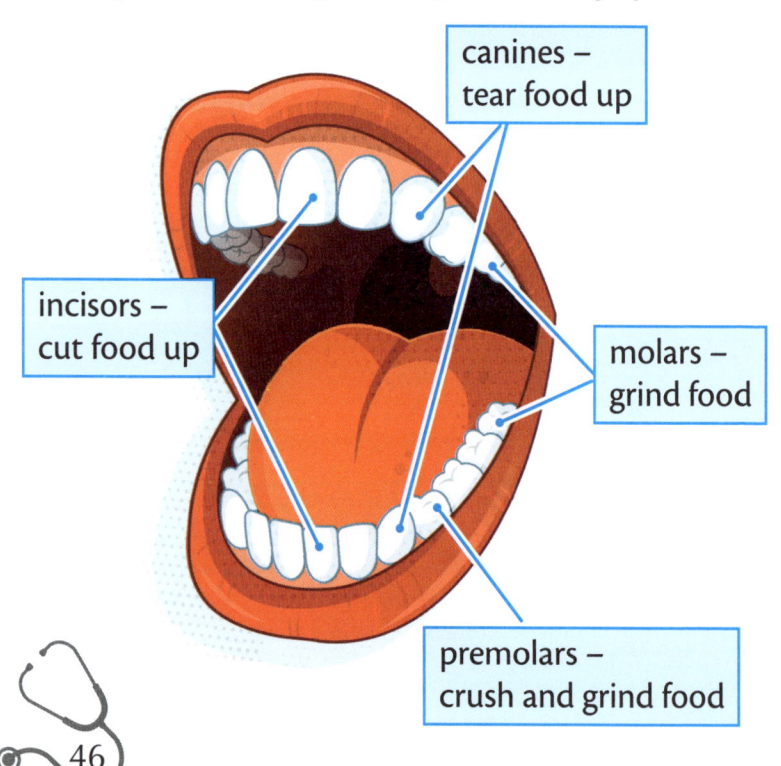

canines – tear food up

incisors – cut food up

molars – grind food

premolars – crush and grind food

2. Oesophagus

Your tongue pushes the food to the back of your mouth, ready for you to swallow. The food then travels down a long tube in your throat, called your oesophagus (say "uh-soh-fuh-guss") and down into your stomach. But it doesn't just slip or slide down by itself. It's squeezed along by strong muscles in your oesophagus, like toothpaste being squeezed out of a tube.

Dr B. Ody's top tip

Take care your food doesn't go down the "wrong way". Your oesophagus is next to your windpipe. (You use your windpipe for breathing.) Usually, a flap of skin covers the top of the windpipe when you swallow. But food sometimes goes down it by mistake and can make you cough.

3. Stomach

In your stomach, your food is churned and mushed some more until it looks like thick, slimy soup. Special juices pour onto it to help break it up. Your stomach's made of strong muscle. It stretches as it fills up. When it's full, it sends messages to your brain to tell you not to eat any more.

Amazing!

Does your tummy rumble when you're hungry? In fact, it can rumble at any time. It's the sound of your digestive system squashing and squeezing. When it's full of food, you can't hear the sounds. When it's empty, it grumbles and growls.

Food stays in your stomach for about two hours while it's being broken down. It takes food around three days to travel right through your body.

49

4. Small intestine

From your stomach, your food is squeezed down into a very long tube, called your small intestine. Here, it is mixed with more juices. Soon it's been broken down enough for nutrients to travel through the tube walls into your blood. Your blood then carries the nutrients around your body to your cells.

Your small intestine is only called "small" because it's not very wide. It's actually as long as a car, coiled up tightly inside you.

Before your blood takes your food to your cells, it heads for your liver. Your liver stores some of the food and gets rid of any poisonous bits.

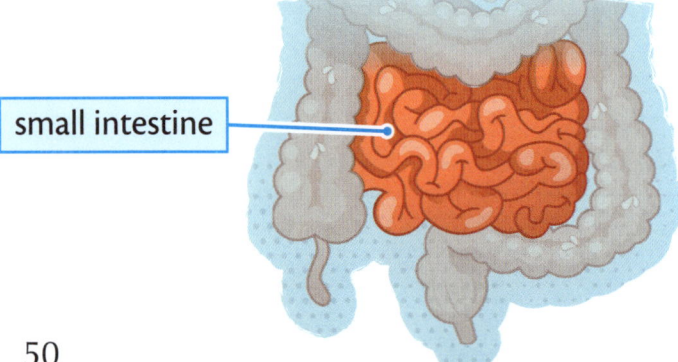

small intestine

5. Large intestine

Any waste food your body can't use goes into your large intestine (it's short but wide). The leftover food clumps together to make a soft lump – poo! It's stored until you go to the toilet and push it out.

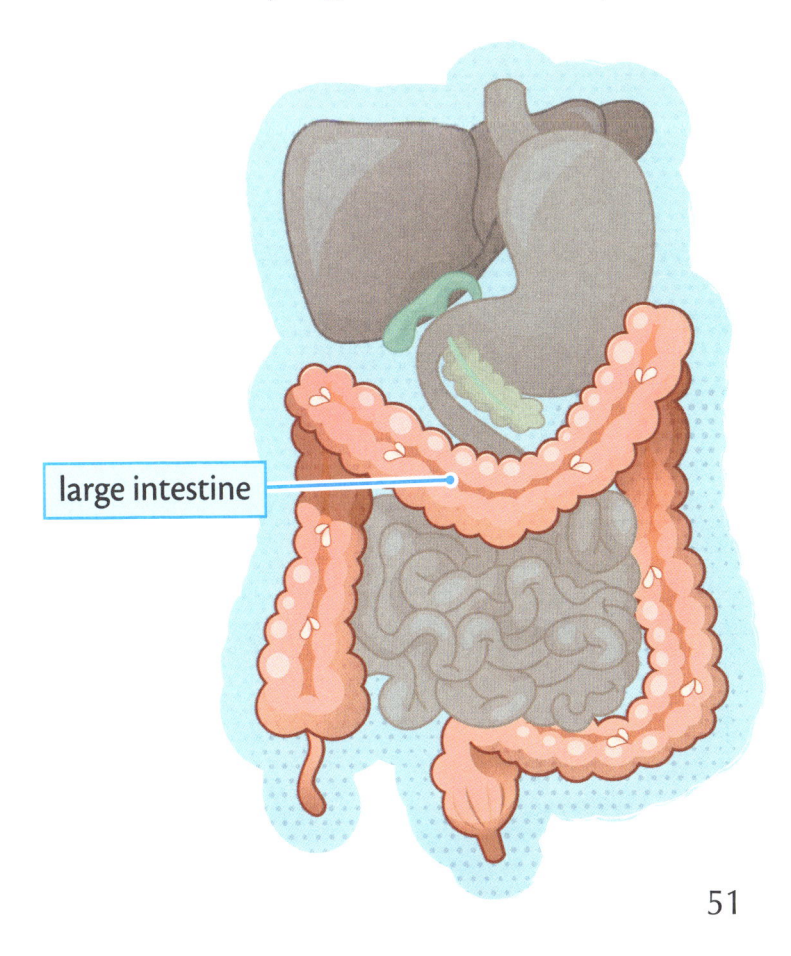

large intestine

Waterworks

Along with **nutritious** food, you need to drink lots of water to stay healthy. Every part of your body needs water to work properly. It helps your body stay at the right temperature, get rid of waste, and keep your joints moving smoothly. Water also helps flush out waste when you go to the toilet.

Low down in your back, you've got two bean-shaped kidneys. Your kidneys aren't part of your digestive system, but they get rid of extra water, and also clean your blood. As blood flows through them, they filter out any waste. They turn the water and waste into urine – it's also called wee.

The urine flows down two tubes into a small, stretchy bag called your bladder. A ring of muscle around the end stops it leaking out.

When you go to the toilet, the muscle relaxes and lets the urine flow out down another tube.

Anyone else need to go now?

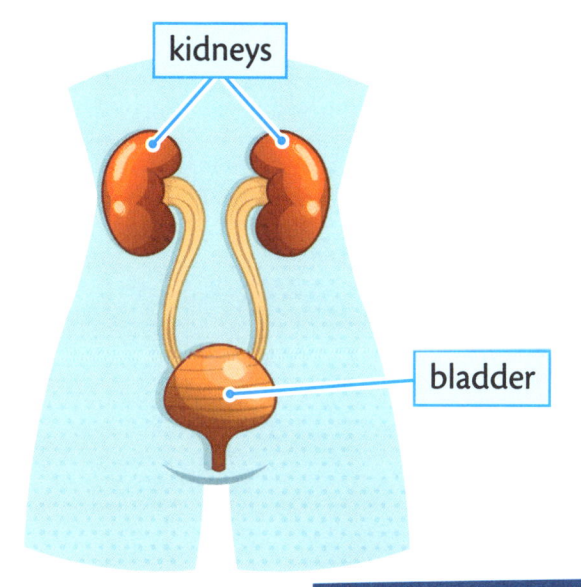

kidneys

bladder

Dr B.Ody's top tip

Check the colour of your wee to see if you're drinking the right amount of water. If it's clear or light yellow, you're drinking enough. If it's darker, you need to drink more.

Amazing!

When it's full, your bladder can hold as much liquid as two cans of drink. But you'd be bursting for the toilet by then!

A great plate?

Eating a balanced diet is the best way of keeping your body in good shape. This means eating a mixture of different kinds of food.

This plate shows you how much of each kind of food it's good to eat. Fill up on fruit and vegetables if you're hungry, and keep sweet and fatty food to a minimum.

fruit and vegetables

starchy food like bread, potatoes and rice

fats and sugars

protein foods like meat, fish, beans and eggs

dairy foods like milk, yoghurt and cheese

55

CHAPTER 5
Brain and nerves

How is everyone feeling? Happy? Full? That's good, because our next stop is the part of your body that controls how you feel, and everything else you do. We're heading up inside your head to your brilliant brain, and it's my favourite bit of the whole tour.

Control centre

Your brain controls every bit of your body, and everything you do, think and feel. How? Well, your body sends information to your brain. Your brain sorts it out and tells your body what to do.
This information zooms around your body along long, thin "wires" called nerves.

Your brain is like an incredibly powerful computer, even though it doesn't look like any computer you've ever seen.

For a start, it's pinky-grey and wobbly, and covered in wrinkles. It's made of billions and billions of nerve cells, all linked together. Blood vessels bring oxygen and nutrients to you brain. Your skull plus a tough cover of skin protects it from harm.

Brain box

Your brain is very precious. Without it, your body wouldn't work at all. It's also very delicate which is why it sits inside your skull. Your skull makes a hard case around it, like a bony crash helmet. It stops your brain getting knocked or bumped. But you'll need to wear a proper helmet as well when you're doing things like riding your bike or playing cricket.

Amazing!

Everyone's brain is about the same size, even if you're a genius and think you know everything!

this is a scan of a person's brain

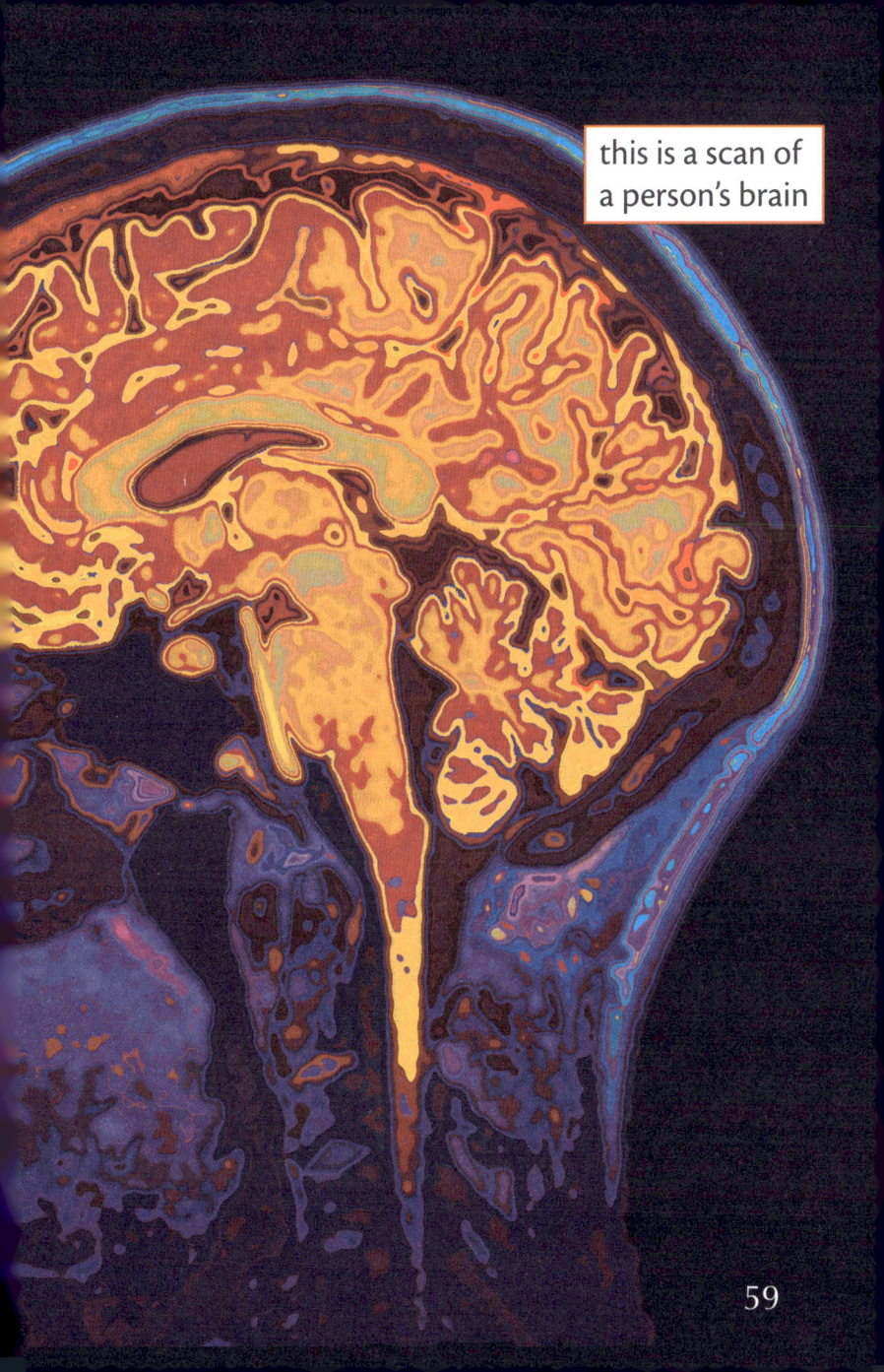

Brain map

Each bit of your brain controls different parts of your body. Your brain is really complicated, and it can be tricky to find your way around it. So, to help you, here is a handy brain map!

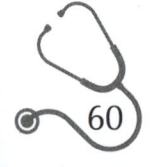

cerebrum
- thinking
- memory
- problem-solving
- learning
- taking in information from our senses
- emotions
- language

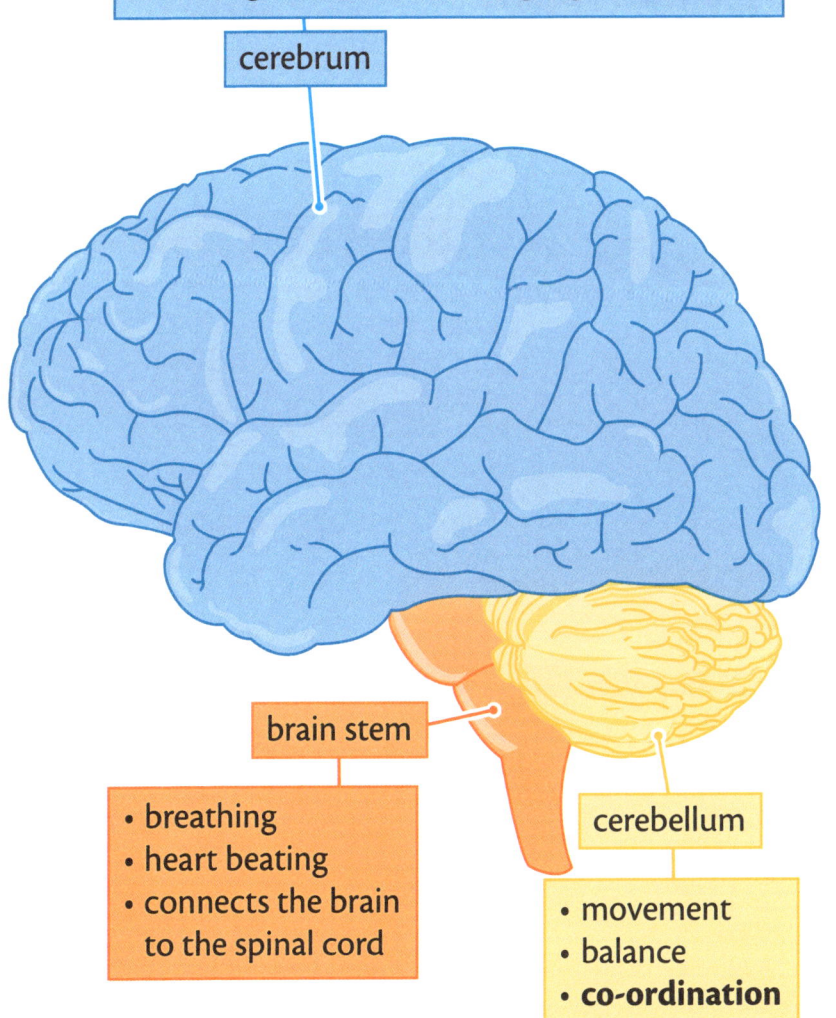

brain stem
- breathing
- heart beating
- connects the brain to the spinal cord

cerebellum
- movement
- balance
- **co-ordination**

Left and right

The majority of people are right-handed, but lots of people are left-handed and a few can use both hands equally. These people are called ambidextrous (say, "am-bee-dex-truss").

Are you left-handed or right-handed?

Scientists once though that it all depended on which half of your brain was in charge. If you were right-handed, they thought it was the left side of your brain that controlled writing and speaking. If you were left-handed, they thought it was the right side. Scientists now think that both sides can work together. We're always learning about our amazing bodies!

Amazing!

A thick strap of around 200 million nerves joins the two halves of your brain together. Messages whizz across it from one side of your brain to the other.

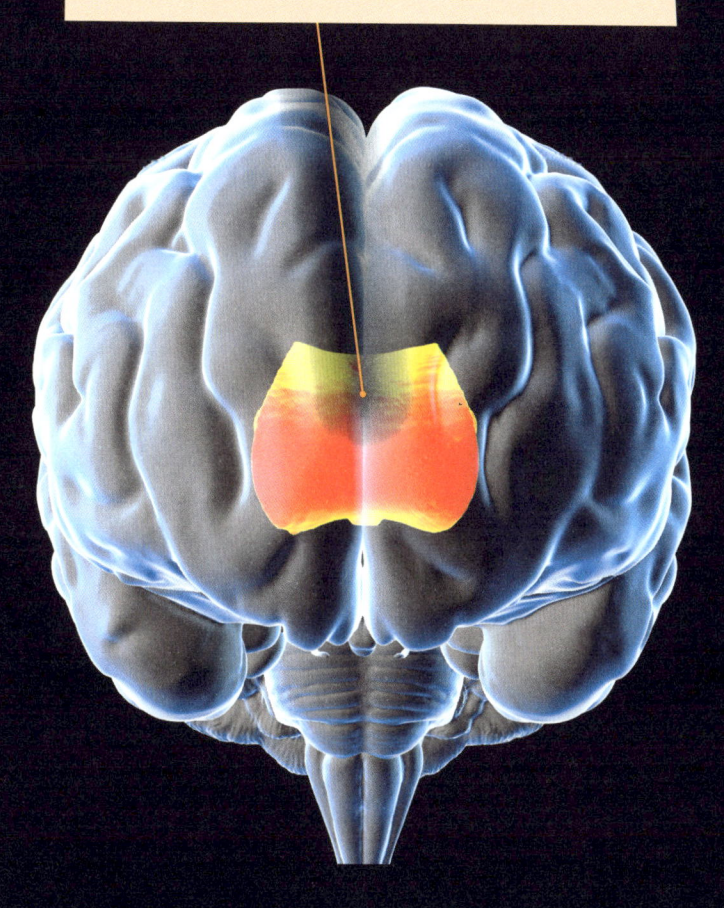

Nervous system

Remember nerves? Those long, thin wires, made from bunches of nerve cells? They link together to carry and pass on messages to and from your brain. Messages from your body tell your brain what's happening. Then messages from your brain tell your body what to do.

A thick bundle of nerves, called your spinal cord, runs down the middle of your back. It goes through your spine and is the main pathway for your nerves. The bones of your spine help to protect the delicate nerves in the cord from harm. Smaller nerves branch off your spinal cord and reach all over your body.

You've got enough nerves in your body to stretch around an Olympic running track almost 200 times.

Amazing!

Some messages race along your nerves faster than a high-speed train.

brain

spinal cord

nerves

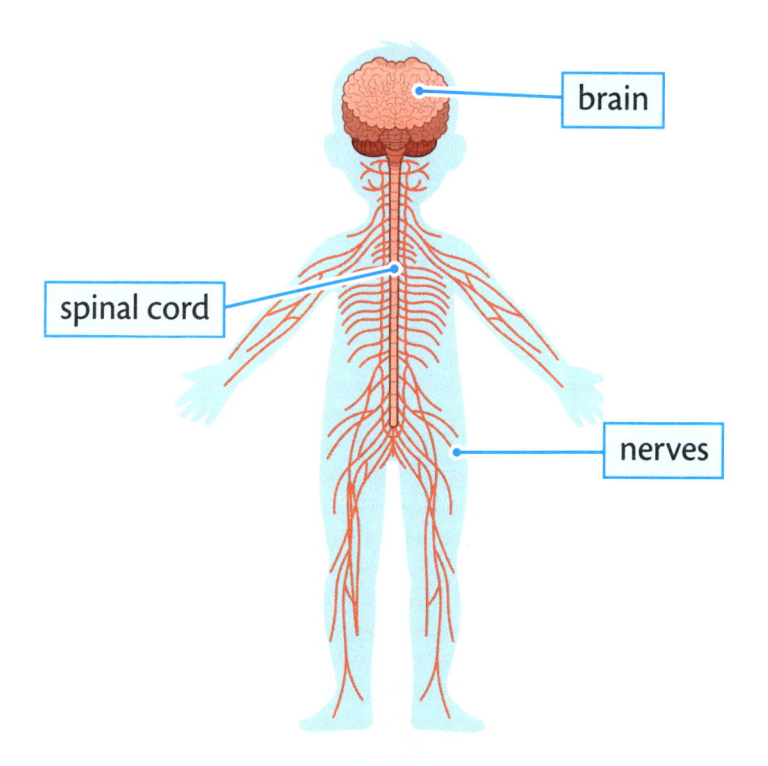

Pins and needles

If you lie on your arm or leg for too long, it can go numb. This is because you've squashed your nerves, and they can't send messages properly. When you take the weight off, you get the tingle of pins and needles. This is a sign that your nerves are getting back to normal.

Time to sleep

After your brain's been hard at work all day, it needs time to rest. It does this while you're asleep. Your body slows down at night, so your brain doesn't have as much to do. Of course, it doesn't stop working altogether. It's far too busy and important for that. It carries on sorting out information from the day. It keeps your heart beating and your lungs breathing. It keeps your body digesting your food. Sleep also gives the rest of your body time to mend and grow. No wonder we spend around a third of our lives asleep!

Amazing!

You need around ten hours of sleep a night. Adults need around seven to eight hours. That's nothing compared to a koala – this sleepy creature spends 18–20 hours napping.

Dr B.Ody's top tip

If I can't get to sleep, I count sheep jumping over a gate. There are lots of other tricks you can try but this one always … works … for … me. Zzzzzzz

Sweet dreams

At times, when you're asleep, your brain bursts into action. Even though your eyes are closed, they may flick quickly back and forth. Your breathing and heart rate go up and down. Experts think this is when you have dreams. Almost everyone dreams, every night. But most of us can't remember what we dreamt about when we wake up in the morning. Can you remember your dreams?

Memory skills

How good is your memory? Try this simple memory game.

Look at the objects in the picture. Then close the book or look away. Say as many things as you can remember.

How many did you remember? Some people naturally have better memories than others. But your memory will get better if you keep practising.

CHAPTER 6
Super senses

Sorry, I must have dropped off (and it looks like I wasn't the only one). I told you counting sheep works wonders, so let's not try doing that again. Now, we've reached the last leg of our tour. It's all about how you make sense of the world around you (and nothing to do with legs, of course).

Making sense

How do you know what's going on around you? How can you tell what a flower looks like or how an ice-cream tastes?

By using your five senses, that's how. Your five senses are seeing, hearing, smelling, tasting and feeling. Each one's linked to a part of your body that sends messages along nerves to your brain.

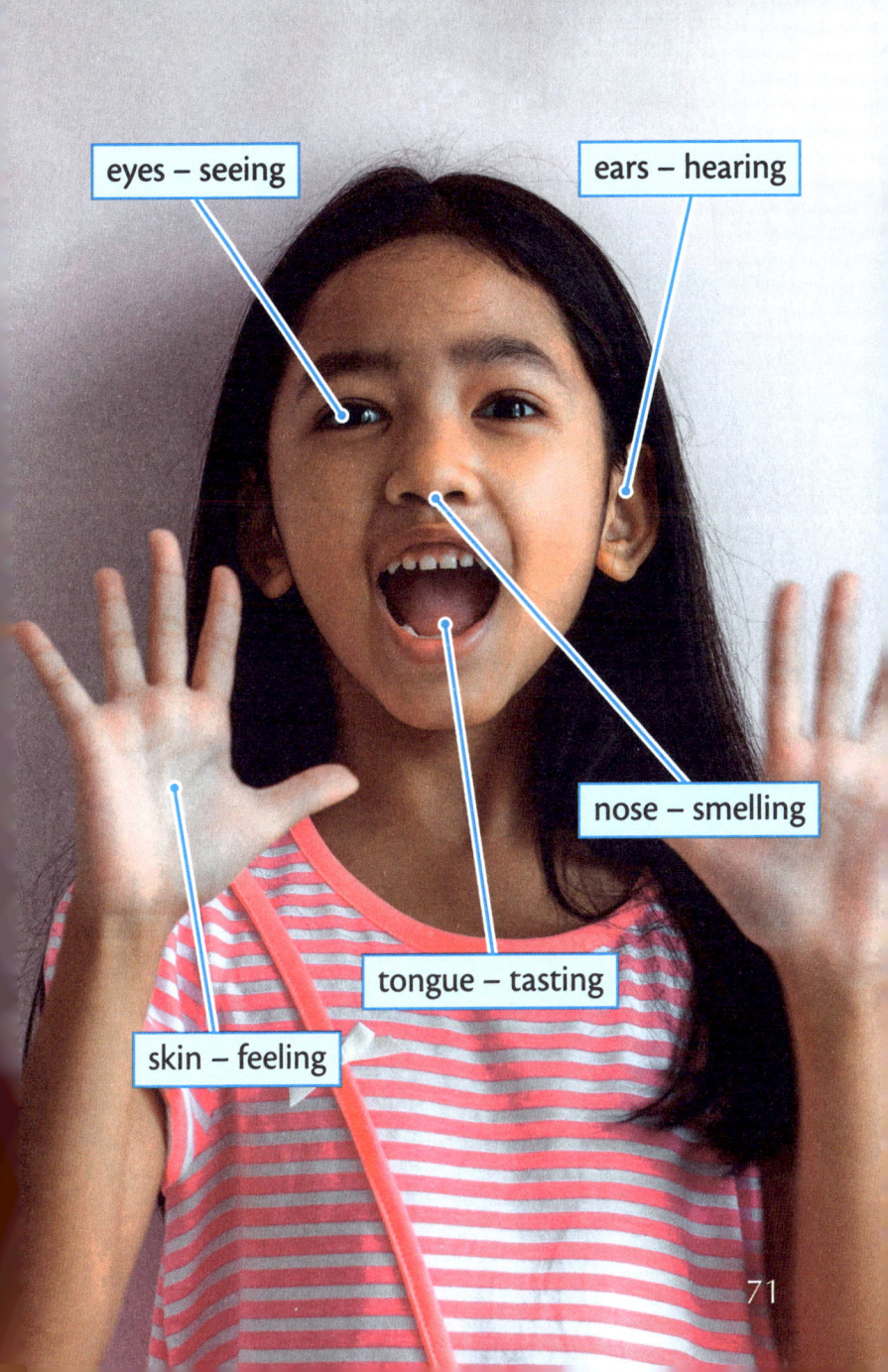

- eyes – seeing
- ears – hearing
- nose – smelling
- tongue – tasting
- skin – feeling

Seeing sense

Your eyes are cleverly designed for seeing. Here's how they work:

1. The little black dots in the centre of your eyes are tiny holes (pupils).
2. They let light into your eyes.
3. The light makes a picture at the back of your eye (retina).
4. Nerves send messages about the picture to your brain.
5. Your brain tells you what you're looking at.

Some of the nerve cells in your eyes help you to see in black and white. Others help you to see in colour.

Amazing!

The picture that appears on your retina is upside-down. Your brain turns it the right way up.

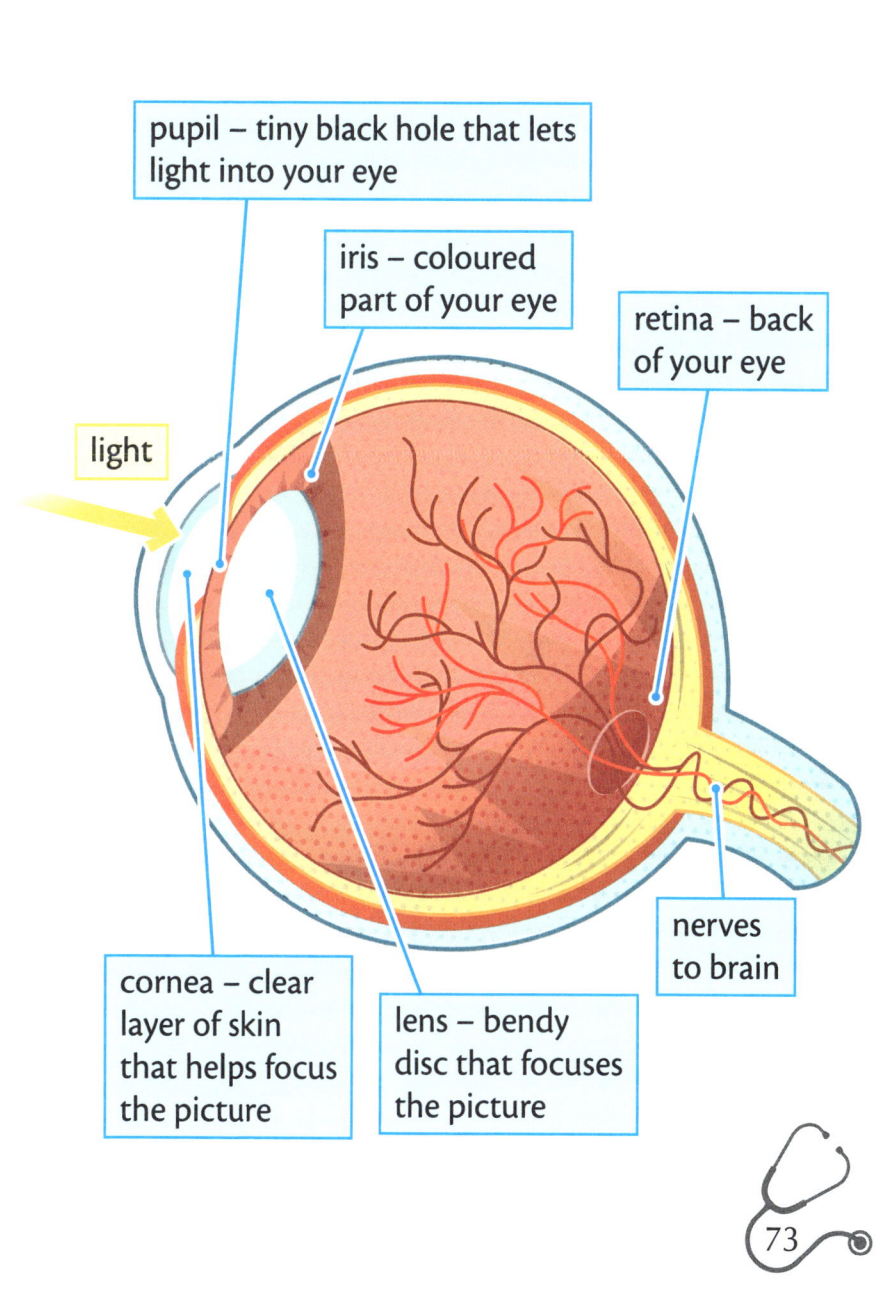

pupil – tiny black hole that lets light into your eye

iris – coloured part of your eye

retina – back of your eye

light

nerves to brain

cornea – clear layer of skin that helps focus the picture

lens – bendy disc that focuses the picture

73

Hear! Hear!

Your ears might look an odd shape, but this makes them brilliant at hearing.

1. Your outer ear sends sounds to the inside of your ear.
2. The sounds travel down a tube and hit a thin piece of skin.
3. They make the skin wobble which sets three tiny bones wobbling, too.
4. Next, the wobbling shakes tiny hairs in a spiral-shaped tube (called the cochlea).
5. The hairs pull on nerves that send messages to your brain.
6. Your brain tells you what you can hear.

Amazing!

The three tiny bones in your ears are only about the same size as grains of rice.

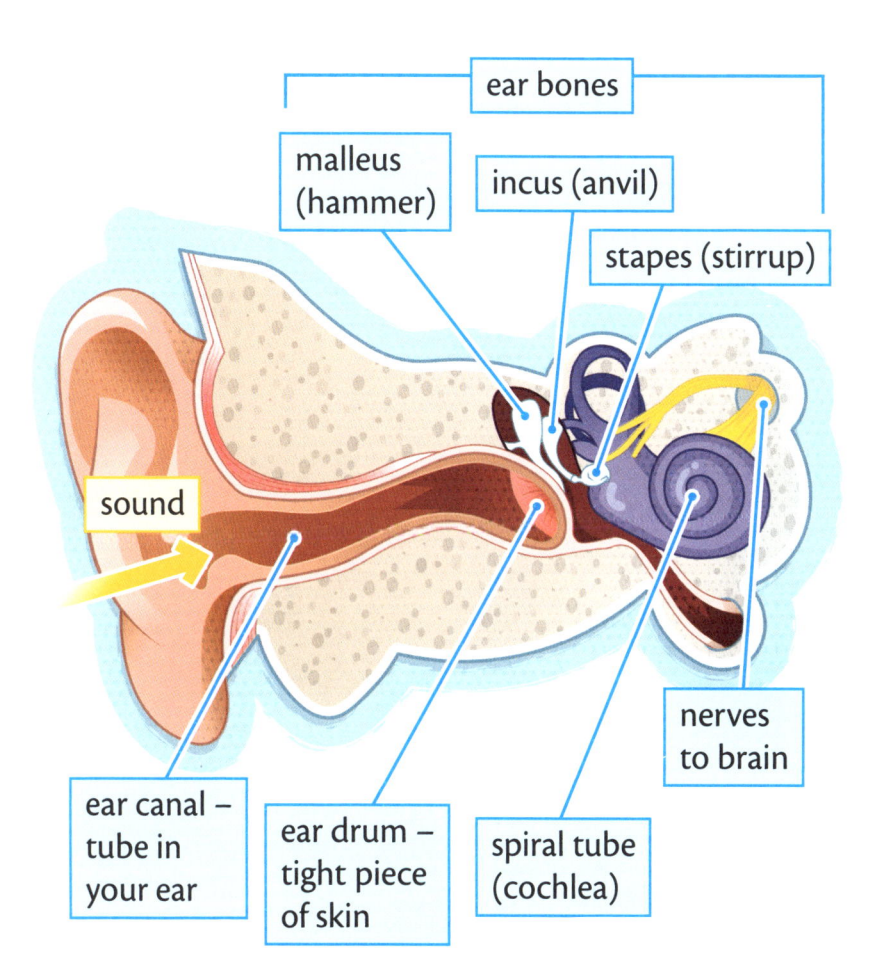

Ear diagram labels:
- ear bones
  - malleus (hammer)
  - incus (anvil)
  - stapes (stirrup)
- sound
- ear canal – tube in your ear
- ear drum – tight piece of skin
- spiral tube (cochlea)
- nerves to brain

Amazing!

An elephant's ears are as big as bedsheets. Apart from hearing, they're used for keeping cool, sending signals and scaring off enemies. Don't you wish YOUR ears could do all that?

Tastes good?

Stick your tongue out and look in the mirror. Can you see that your tongue's covered in little bumps?

Inside these bumps are your taste buds. They pick up flavour from your food and send messages along nerves to your brain. Your tongue can pick up five main different tastes – sweet, salty, bitter, sour and savoury.

Tasting doesn't just tell you if your food is good to eat. It also warns you if food is bad or has gone off and could make you ill. The bumps also contain sensitive cells that tell you if your food is hot or cold.

You've got around 8,000 taste buds on your tongue. You've also got them on the inside of your cheeks and on your lips.

taste bud

Amazing!

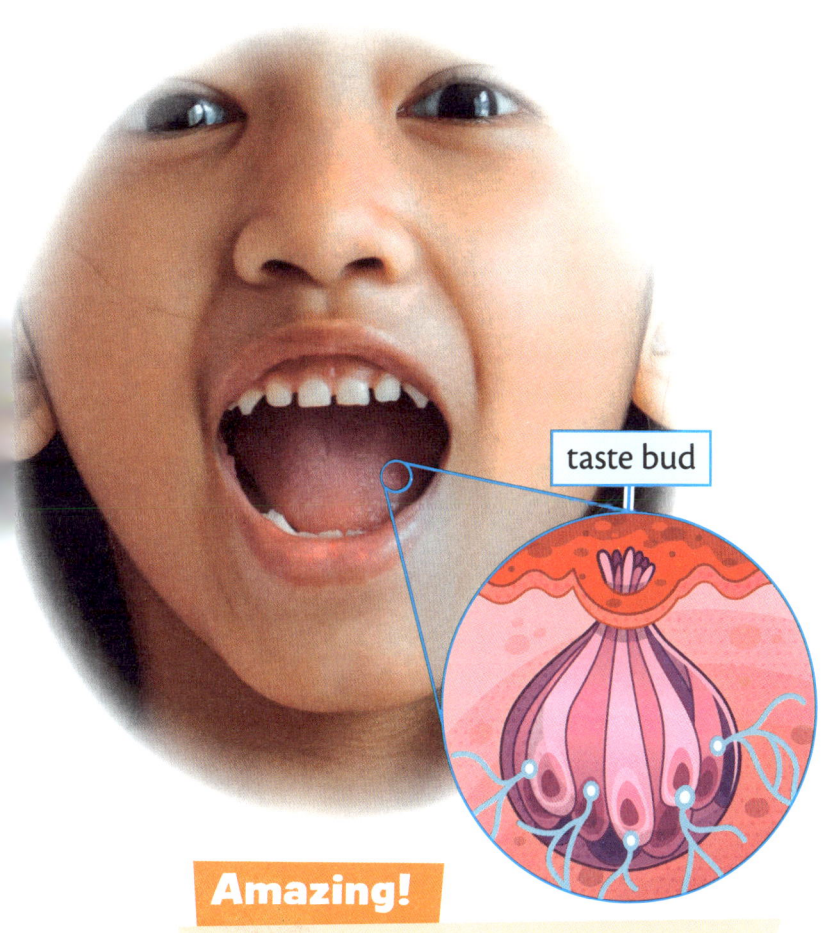

A giraffe's tongue is as long as your arm and ... dark purple! The colour stops the tongue getting sunburnt when it's sticking out to pluck leaves from the trees to eat.

Smells terrible?

Smells float in the air. You can't see them, but you know they're there.

Smells go up your nose when you breathe in. Special **receptors** send messages about the smells to your brain. Some things smell lovely, like a bunch of flowers. Others smell terrible, like old socks. Like taste, smell can also tell you if food is good to eat or not.

Smells are stronger when you sniff. Usually, you only take in a small amount of air (and smells) when you breathe in. But sniffing pulls in lots more air (and smells) into your nose.

Your sense of smell and taste work together. So, if your nose is bunged up with a cold, even a yummy piece of cake can taste like cardboard.

nerves

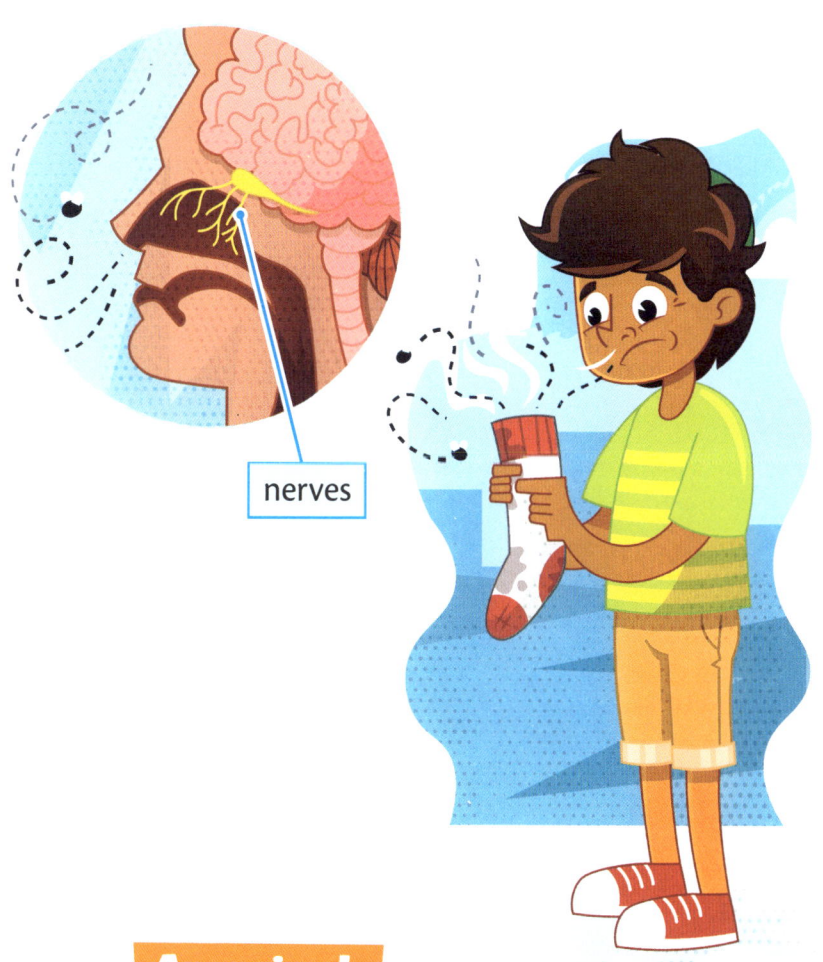

Amazing!

You can sniff out around one trillion smells but a dog can smell 10,000 times better than you!

Touchy-feely

Alongside all its other jobs, your skin lets you touch and feel things. Packed under the surface of your skin are millions of tiny nerves. They send messages to your brain. Then your brain tells you if things feel hot or cold, soft or hard, rough or smooth, or painful.

Amazing!

Your skin's not the same all over. It's most sensitive on your fingertips, lips and toes.

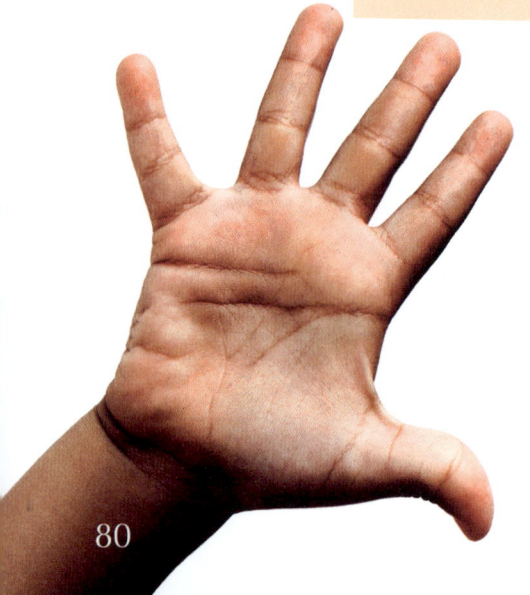

Congratulations! You've reached the end of the tour. I hope you've enjoyed it. I know I have. Make sure you look after your brilliant body. It's the only one you've got, and it works hard all your life. Now, I don't know about you lot but I'm off for a nice, long rest! Please take a certificate on the way out. You've earned it.

Tricks of the senses

How sharp are your senses? Here are two tests to try …

1. Close your eyes and touch your nose. Can you do it first time? Can your fingers find your nose without you having to look? Your body always seems to know where each bit of you is.

2. Look at the picture. Which line looks longer? In fact, they're both the same length but your eyes sometimes play tricks on your brain. Instead of seeing things as they really are, your brain sees different shapes or colours.

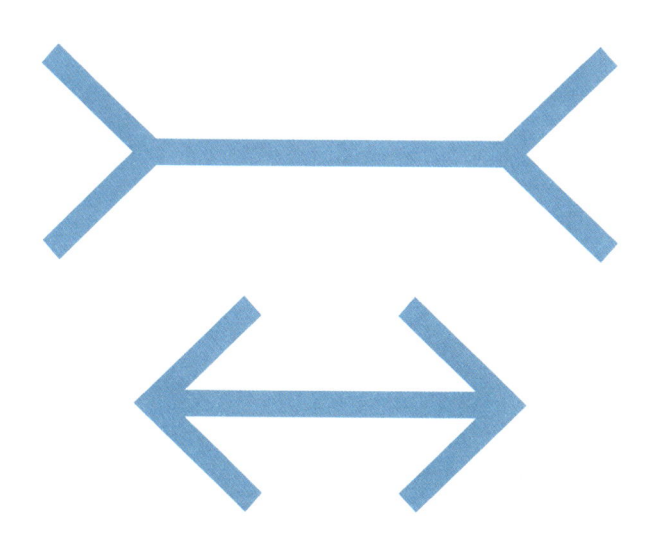

Glossary

automatically without thinking about what you're doing

blood vessels tiny tubes that carry blood around your body

cells tiny building blocks of your body

clenched closed in a tight ball

clot lump of blood that has stuck together

co-ordination being able to move different parts of your body at the same time

delicate soft and easy to hurt or harm

follicle tube-shaped hole in skin

germs tiny living things that can cause illness

gland part of the body that makes things like sweat and oil

marrow jelly-like tissue inside some of your bones

membrane thin, stretchy skin over something

microscope a scientific tool that makes things look bigger

mites tiny spider-like creatures

nerves long, thin fibres that pass messages between your brain and other parts of your body

nutritious full of the good parts of food your body needs

nutrients good parts of food your body needs

oxygen gas from the air that we need to breathe

ridges fine lines on our fingertips

receptors cells that receive information such as smells

scab hard, dry patch that covers a wound

scalp the skin on the top of your head

small intestine part of the long tube your food goes down

supple able to move easily

About the author

A bit about me ….

Hi, I'm Anita, and I'm very happy to meet you. I live in the north of England with my husband, children and dogs. I like reading, writing and playing tennis. Sometimes, I dream that I've won Wimbledon. I love exploring different places, when I'm not on a body tour. I also love knitting, though no one in my family wants to wear the things I make for them!

Anita Ganeri

Why did you want to be an author?

I've always loved writing, and languages in general. It's so satisfying when you write something that works well and sounds good. I never planned on becoming an author, though. Like many things in life, I fell into it by accident. I was working in London for some well-known publishers of children's books, and it went from there. Being an author isn't always easy, but I feel extremely lucky to spend my time doing something I really like.

Why did you want to write this book?

My dad was a doctor, and we always had a human skull (not a real one) in the back of our car. I think it was called Sidney, but I may be making that bit up. I was so proud of my dad, and sorry that I didn't follow in his footsteps. However, I find the human body fascinating, and I especially like the long and technical words, even when I don't know what they mean.

Do you have a favourite fact from the book?

All of my favourite facts from the book are about the brain. It is incredible that a pinkish, jelly-like lump can control everything we do, think, say, and who we are.

What do you think the most amazing thing about the human body is?

That it all works together, even though it has so many different parts. When you think about it, it's amazing that all the parts know their own jobs but also work together.

What do you hope readers will get out of this book?

I hope that they will get a sense of how brilliant a human body is. I hope they'll find it funny and full of fascinating facts. And I hope they like Dr B. Ody – even if he keeps dropping off to sleep!

About the illustrator

What made you want to be an illustrator?

I probably started drawing before I even started talking. For as long as I can remember, I have loved picture books, reading comics, watching cartoons and playing video games. Being able to tell stories through images made me want to be an illustrator.

Diego Vaisberg

What did you like best about illustrating this book?

I worked on this book side-by-side with Lu Pérez Pizá who created Dr B. Ody and imagined all the fun characters. I enjoyed working on such a challenging and fun project, and being able to discover more about the human body.

What was the most difficult thing about illustrating this book?

The most challenging part of illustrating this book was making sure the human body was accurate, whilst maintaining a fun element.

Do you prefer illustrating fiction or non-fiction books?
I enjoy illustrating both fiction and non-fiction, but I always prefer fiction books, because we can create new worlds and characters.

Did you learn anything while illustrating this book?
I learned a lot about how the body works. I was fascinated to learn how to cure hiccups, a piece of information I found extremely useful, especially as I often suffer from them.

What do you think is the most amazing thing about the human body?
What has always surprised me is how our brain can control several actions at the same time. Something as simple as lifting something heavy, makes several muscles work together. While we think about where to put the heavy object, we are also blinking and breathing and doing lots of other things without thinking about it. It's amazing how the entire human body is connected.

Have you ever broken a bone?
Luckily, I have never broken any bones. I have sprained my ankle while playing football with friends, another of my passions.

Book chat

Before you started reading, what did you think the book would be like? Were you right?

What have you learnt from reading this book?

If you could ask the author one question, what would you ask?

What's the most surprising or amazing thing you have learnt from the book?

If you had to describe the book in one sentence, what would you say?

How do you feel about your body now you've read this book?

What might you do differently having read this book?

If you could give the author one piece of advice to improve the book, what would it be?

If you had to think of a new title for this book, what would you call it?

Would you recommend this book? Why or why not?

Book challenge:
Draw a picture and some labels for the part of the body tour you found most interesting.

Collins
BIG CAT

Published by Collins
An imprint of HarperCollins*Publishers*

The News Building
1 London Bridge Street
London
SE1 9GF
UK

Macken House
39/40 Mayor Street Upper
Dublin 1
D01 C9W8
Ireland

© HarperCollins*Publishers* Limited 2024

10 9 8 7 6 5 4 3 2 1

ISBN 978-0-00-868118-0

All rights reserved. No part of this publication may be reproduced, stored in a retrieval system, or transmitted in any form by any means, electronic, mechanical, photocopying, recording or otherwise, without the prior written permission of the Publisher or a licence permitting restricted copying in the United Kingdom issued by the Copyright Licensing Agency Ltd, 5th Floor, Shackleton House, 4 Battle Bridge Lane, London SE1 2HX.

British Library Cataloguing-in-Publication Data
A catalogue record for this publication is available from the British Library.

Download the teaching notes and word cards to accompany this book at: http://littlewandle.org.uk/signupfluency/

Get the latest Collins Big Cat news at
collins.co.uk/collinsbigcat

Author: Anita Ganeri
Illustrators: Diego Vaisberg with Lu Pérez Pizá, DGPH Studio (Advocate Art)
Publisher: Laura White
Product manager: Caroline Green
Series editor: Charlotte Raby
Development editor: Catherine Baker
Commissioning editor: Suzannah Ditchburn
Project manager: Emily Hooton
Copyeditor: Sally Byford
Proofreader: Catherine Dakin
Cover designer: Sarah Finan
Typesetter: 2Hoots Publishing Services Ltd
Production controller: Katharine Willard

Printed in the UK.

MIX
Paper | Supporting responsible forestry
FSC™ C007454

This book is produced from independently certified FSC™ paper to ensure responsible forest management.

For more information visit: www.harpercollins.co.uk/green

Made with responsibly sourced paper and vegetable ink

Scan to see how we are reducing our environmental impact.

Acknowledgements
The publishers gratefully acknowledge the permission granted to reproduce the copyright material in this book. Every effort has been made to trace copyright holders and to obtain their permission for the use of copyright material. The publishers will gladly receive any information enabling them to rectify any error or omission at the first opportunity.

p6l Jose Luis Calvo/Shutterstock, p6r W.Y. Sunshine/Shutterstock, p7t Barou abdennaser/Shutterstock, p7c Cones/Shutterstock, p7b Jose Luis Calvo/Shutterstock, p9 Piotr Velixar/Shutterstock, p12tl Zurijeta/Shutterstock, p12tr Leestudio/Shutterstock, p12bl Eric Isselee/Shutterstock, p12br Svietlieishyi Andrii/Shutterstock, p13 rSnapshotPhotos/Shutterstock, p14l Fleckstone/Shutterstock, p14r Artemiya/Shutterstock, p15l Leestudio/Shutterstock, p15r Wirestock Creators/Shutterstock, p21 Natallia Yaumenenka/Shutterstock, p28tl Roman Samborskyi/Shutterstock, p28tr PV productions/Shutterstock, p28b Krakenimages.com/Shutterstock, p32 Alfred Pasieka/Science Photo Library, p35 NIBSC/Science Photo Library, p37 Atstock Productions/Shutterstock, p49 Marian Weyo/Shutterstock, pp58–59 SpeedKingz/Shutterstock, p61 Rauf pessel/Shutterstock, p63 Kateryna Kon/Shutterstock, p66 Manuk/Shutterstock, p68tl Lucie Lang/Shutterstock, p68tr Givaga/Shutterstock, p68b Tobibambola/Shutterstock, p69t Valkoinen/Shutterstock, p69c Grey_and/Shutterstock, p69b Olga Guchek/Shutterstock, p71 & 77 Ranee Sornprasitt/Alamy, p80 Cunaplus/Shutterstock.